COUNTING YOU TO PIECES

Michelle Ahern Bevans

This is an IndieMosh book

brought to you by MoshPit Publishing
an imprint of Mosher's Business Support Pty Ltd

PO Box 147
Hazelbrook NSW 2779

indiemosh.com.au

Copyright © Michelle Ahern Bevans 2020

The moral right of the author has been asserted in accordance with the Copyright Amendment (Moral Rights) Act 2000.

All rights reserved. Except as permitted under the Australian Copyright Act 1968 (for example, fair dealing for the purposes of study, research, criticism or review) no part of this publication may be reproduced, stored in a retrieval system, or transmitted in any form or by any means, electronic, mechanical, photocopying, recording or otherwise, without the written permission of the publisher.

 A catalogue record for this work is available from the National Library of Australia

https://www.nla.gov.au/collections

Title:	Counting You to Pieces
Author:	Ahern Bevans, Michelle (1979–)
ISBNs:	978-1-922440-17-4 (paperback) 978-1-922440-18-1 (ebook – epub) 978-1-922440-19-8 (ebook – mobi)
Subjects:	POETRY / General; Women Authors

No individual in these poems is taken from real life. Any resemblance to any person or persons living or dead is accidental and unintentional. The author, their agents and publishers cannot be held responsible for any claim otherwise and take no responsibility for any such coincidence.

Extract from "Mirror"
Crossing the Water by Sylvia Plath. Copyright © 1960 Ted Hughes. Used by permission of HarperCollins Publishers. (US)

Collected Poems by Sylvia Plath used with permission from 'Faber and Faber Ltd publishers (UK and worldwide)

"Crazy Love, Vol. II"
Words and music by Paul Simon. © Songs Of Universal, Inc./Universal/MCA Music Publishing Pty. Ltd. All rights reserved. International copyright secured. Reprinted with permission.

Cover concept by Michelle Ahern Bevans
Cover design and layout by Ally Mosher at allymosher.com
Cover images from Envato Elements

Author photo by Annie McKay

"Somebody could walk into this room
And say your life is on fire
It's all over the evening news
All about the fire in your life
On the evening news"

Paul Simon, *Crazy Love II*

*"She rewards me with tears and an agitation of hands.
I am important to her. She comes and goes.
Each morning it is her face that replaces the darkness.
In me she has drowned a young girl, and in me an old woman
Rises toward her day after day, like a terrible fish."*

Sylvia Plath, *Mirror*

*For my parents,
Barry and Coleen*

Contents

Blue	1
Shush	2
Trip, Not	4
Now	6
Beautiful Breakable	7
(W)hole	8
Rain Like This	9
Unmother	10
Sting	11
Tom's Diner	12
Up in Smoke	13
Pages	14
Tomorrow After Tuesday	15
All Mouth and No Trousers	16
Sliced	18
Harbour View	19
Autumn	20
Short Message Service	21
Sink	22
It's You or the Rain	23
Boxed	24
Schlept	26

Lucid Boy	27
Here's To You	28
tiptoe	30
Him	31
Back	33
Moss Veil	34
Empyrean	35
Suburbia	36
Beatrice	38
Fuckin' Jesus Christ	39
Plip	40
Tidal Wave	41
Someone's Daughter	42
Golden Girl	44
Tennessee	46
Tree	48
Complete	49
About the Author	51

Blue

A blue light streaked
naked across my line of sight
leaving me coloured pink
just for the sake of love's dirty fingers
left
tracing circles across my belly

Shush

Someday
She will be exposed colour and light
Gathering like white
Woven cotton

Softly
Moving room to room
Feet bare
Upon these floors

Static
Will whirr and buzz
Him
Awake

Stirring
Heavy pots
Laden with lust
Served from the opposite ends of a long timber table

(Vacant halls)
Separating
Their desires
With silverware and white
Woven cotton

Trip, Not

Lost in the foibles of life
I found your shadow   o u t s t r e t c h e d
On the footpath –
Lucky I didn't trip on my brown laces

You had me lulled into a false sense of comedy

5 – Counting You To Pieces

Now

A narrative of therapy
Unravelled –
The probabilities were endless

Sleepless endings
Punctured the air
Awake

Dim confusion has its way
While the world
Sits damp with wonder
Blinking

Thick, the air
Like heat
Like hate
Like heaven

The glare of gold on
Ebb and flow
And endless probabilities
Are strangling

Beautiful Breakable

Peculiar hearts clashed together in an awkward fumble

Desperate for lust to turn to love –

And so capable of

Destruction between the sheets

(W)hole

His vacant stare need not be replaced by her empty smile

Rain Like This

Rain falls tight against the air

Tickling the ground as it lands.

Tresses of hair fall around her face

As guided hands steal flesh from the bone.

Squeezing tight,

Pinching her pink with delight

She lands like the rain –

With her heart between his teeth

And he's biting down hard.

Unmother

The fucking unmotherness of it all

The expanse of cunt
Spreading its legs
Wide around your ears

Your eyes blackened
With disappointment

Hope in softness, betrayed in tightness
Fingertips brush your chest
And you flinch

What a cunt can do

Sting

The hot hum of electricity
Murmurs
And silences the chatter

A muted haze drapes
Below the cloud
Sucking heat into our lungs
And sighing with sweat

The sting of Spring
Hopeful and neurotic

Morning light
Swollen with promise
Playful –
Tiptoes
Toward us

Tom's Diner

They smile,
A toothy grin from one and all.
"To absent friends," they chimed.

Glancing 'round, they noticed he'd left.

Up in Smoke

This city is saturated with you
And I want it to catch fire
And burn itself to the ground.
The heaving walls of the buildings
Suck and blow at me
As the wind whips around your corners.
Running breathlessly
I trip on your shadows,
Clambering to my feet
I'm dodging cars – afraid of the sound they'll make
As they crash into my bones.

Pages

Hid amongst the colours of the day

So I could find you,

So I could shade you

Black to white,

Left to right

Amongst the pages of the day

Tomorrow After Tuesday

She tiptoes toward you
Giggling
The white shag pile rug squishes beneath
Her berry-scented toes

A delighted twirl as she falls to the couch –
A playful landing placing her between
Tanned leather and soft puppy fur

She nuzzles
He cowls
Together they share

More than a moment

A memory
Burrowing down deep
To days when she has a choice

To rise above –
Terrifyingly beyond
You all

All Mouth and No Trousers

(And other quips from loves lost)

Distance makes the arse go yonder
Equipped with bad hair and rabbit teeth
What the fuck did I know?
And was that going to stop me

Plump with hope and self-affectation
I was certain I deserved
Better than this (you)

Grinning in to polaroids
Squinting at the sun under straw hats
Sipping cider on rolling hills
Motor cars roaring past

A road trip from England to France
Across countryside I didn't understand
Or pause to listen to

Faces and places
Erases
Me
Marvelling at the back of your head

Scanning the contents of my suitcase
Scattered across a white quilt set somewhere
Between Paris and Fuck This
A gold zip bag
Holding toothbrush, sunscreen
My dignity

Departed as quickly as you did
Over the edge of the towering balcony
Streets below now holding your fists

Leaving me
Holding the camera – polaroid snapped
Fading through

Sliced

I see your face alive in a sea of ferociousness

Anger in your burning eyes

Crashing into me

Slicing me open like fruit.

Sucking back your breath

Leaving me wet

And my mind awake with the heat.

Harbour View

A palatable silence creeps its way
Around corners
Until you're lurched upon in a dark room,
Wearing only your grandfather's underpants
And a waist-coat from your first marriage.

Autumn

Fold me down

And push me flat.

A weighted world heaves me to the ground

Landing –

With dirt in my hair and

Leaves falling into my mouth.

Drowning the life out of me,

Stuffing me with your breath.

Short Message Service

He thought I hated him
because I did not respond
To his comments about cunts.
How sweet.

Sink

Submerging faces from my life

Sink

Escaping bubbles of breath

Speeling upwards,

And I hope they're

Drowning not waving

It's You or the Rain

Nights are a vast empty ocean
Filled with crashing dreams
And murmurs of faces

While away,
I'll while away

Masking the night
With thunderous clouds
And a pouring madness
Until it's you

Boxed

A lick of cloth,
Puff of dust
Scissors slice open the belly of your past
Insides turned out – Laid bare
Bones clattering in the afternoon breeze
As you wade, elbow-deep in memories

Like a familiar friend
Or discarded parts of a child's toy
Scattered now
After being boxed and bound all these years.

Thrust into the mind of a stranger:
A teenager, wide-eyed
Desperately unawake to the boredom of reality
Sky-high expectations tower above you like
An immense empire

Oh you will clamber and conquer
The almighty oomph of the ordinary
Will not touch your tides
Bounding building to building,
Tinkering with wonder above the clouds
Oh you will reign, life supreme.
Old friend.

Schlept

Can I write about your faces
Trounced in a sea of ferociousness

Adrift on an isolated moment
Slicing every swift and sudden epoch of the mind

In a streaming line of consciousness –

A moment in her hands
Leaves your mind awake for days

Lucid Boy

Thinking moments into days
She swallowed what was left

Pausing – tea pot tilted
Starring lazily across the kitchen table
Recalling his lucid smiles

Hearing contentment in her breath,
Reminding her of the hollowness
She has no need to face

Here's To You

Awake

Ears pounding with silence –

An echo chamber from a noisy dream.

The air damp and heavy with you,

Memories now scattered around the room

Like underwear

Reaching

I could not place you –

Not now, not then.

A time when the place was us

And your broad chest was an expanse of country

To explore

Remembering

You on your knee in the bar that night,

For show and free drinks of course –

The rapture of onlookers

As we pretended our love away

Those large brutish hands
Scooping mine
As your elbows crashed into your dinner plate
And you reached across the table
To say...

Words
I could not hear
Through the din of the room
Or the decade that passed

A corridor of chaos
Tunnels us back
To memories tucked in the creases of your eyes -
And the remembering self
Is craving

tiptoe

around the matter
indefinitely

who needs the fucking past
or whatever you have
to hold
for future days

anyway?

I watched and waited
for that bus

and you

but you didn't look back
and the review mirror is covered in mud
and this ticket stub ain't worth nothing

dear driver

Him

Some days I'd get lost
amongst the pages and folds
of your skin.
It was desperation that stole your glance
as you looked away to another world.
Sudden eyes dart back as passion rises like
a beast within
and I feel you
hot against my mouth.

"It's the least I can do,"
I lied as I turned and walked back to my room.

Is it? Is it really the least?
Surely the least is nothing. Nothing at all.

Back

Sprawled there, your warm body
Tilted upwards
Offered like a god –
Taken like a desperate animal

Your skin pinched between my fingers
And clamped beneath my teeth
Sweat, matting my hair
As my tongue tangled
Itself around you
Tasting your stories and sliding over your voice
Punctuating your accent with moisture

Air pounded hard against my ears
Breath roaring inside my head
The heat rose
Inhaling you inside my cheeks
Chest tight with air

Curtains drift
Daylight breaks
Glasses clank on the carpet
Rolling against one another, empty

Moss Veil

Wearing today
Slumped over my shoulders
Like a heavy winter coat
Buttons open
Fur collar prodding my ear lobes

Brown leaves
Curl and furl
Around the grass
At my feet

Today is tired
And helpless

Feet walk me
Heart warms me
Air awaits
And clarity calms my eyes

Empyrean

Marching forward
Watching life creep backward

The flames and dangling wire
drape across the horizon

The smell of disgust burns the inside of my nostrils and
Shadows deafen the dust as they move across the night

Watching, blood slowly seeps under the door –
Leaving this room empty and still and beating.

Suburbia

The bitumen sparkles
Specks of gold dance on black
The rising road towers
In front of the dashboard

Jolted down in fistfuls – the car window opens
Revealing the scene:
Fibro peeled and cracked
Red brick sturdy and sullen

Right foot twinges as it shifts
From carpet to accelerator
Arch lifts
Toes gripping tight on rubber thongs

Sunshine beams across the street
Like a wheel-of-fortune assistant
Desperate to make the showcase look appealing
Fingers s t r e t c h e d

Here to the left – all of this could be yours:
Red bin, letterbox, concrete driveway
And here to the right: but wait, there's more:
TV antenna, neighbours' Corolla, wired flyscreens

The cul-de-sac wraps around
Handbrake
Headshake

Beatrice

"Believe me not!" she cried,
As Shakespeare's last real heroine
Slumped to the floor in a pool of Elizabethan beige
Then consoled herself with thoughts
of taking a career in politics.

Fuckin' Jesus Christ

"1100 billion light years old," he chuffed.
"Honestly, darling, I am."
The prophet of Jesus you did not know.
Mounted in the church, amongst my friends,
I heal no wounds and change no wine –
I am the sickness in your head.

Plip

Rolling thoughts

Glazed over by two windows afloat on the world

A desperate angst awaits you

As you sleep inside a mindlessness of

Sad that just won't stop.

Tidal Wave

You're everywhere at once
The world has an extra heart beat
And it's helping me keep time
Your face has changed

Bridges and boundaries
Crossed and off

Crying on the 380
Miles from nowhere

Someone's Daughter

Seems the truth hitchhiked its way out of town
Long ago, for you
Dear one.

Or was it kidnapped?
Bundled
Dusty and dry –
Slung
Into the utility tray
Of a pickup truck

Coarse rope woven between its ankles,
Gasping for air
As the truck sped westward
Highway-bound
Gagged and generous
In lies

~ ~ ~

How beautiful the world will be
As I build it brick by brick –
Made-to-measure manipulation

I'll carve a seat to nestle and nest
Wicker wickedness
Cradling my fragile ego

Feeding morsels to muppets
They'll learn to survive
As I craft the stories
And write their lives

Stuffing envelopes with letters
I've invented the proof
And licked stamps to seal –
It's the truth

The stream of bullshit I've made
Could carry tall ships to sea
As I curl up and hide
Inside my made-up family

Golden Girl

Two dimples greet me
In the afternoon sun

They're always first up out of their seat
Like an eager handshake

Beaming – that sun and you
A giggle

Arms thrust
Blonde hair squeezes between us

Sipping the day away through straws and strawberries
It's telling this truth, this time

I feel completed in ways I'm
not ready to be finished

45 – Counting You To Pieces

Tennessee

It was a secret
All of this
Because of you

I'm running across the yard
From you
Over the road to the neighbours' house
From you

Barefoot springing up the steep drive
You might see through our bedroom window
I can move quick
From you

Scrawling nonsense
Hiding from you
I'll duck under the covers
Laughing with you
I'll sneak across the wirey carpet
Toward you
I'll leap cushion to cushion
Bouncing with you

Crocodiles in the water
A snap or a slap

Trampoline high
We fly

We drove thousands of kilometres across desert
Dirt and dust – not a car for days
An exercise book, ruled with grids
Pen poised – I'm waiting for the numbers
To count us down to Uluru

Tearing, so slowly
Mintee wrappers
Making curtains
To keep us in

An expanse of night outside the caravan
We giggle
But a pinched lip is coming my way
I just know it

Tree

I held the sky
in the corner of my eye
while I counted you to pieces

I left when I got to 17
and caught a cab home in the rain

Complete

1, 3, 5, 7, 9, 11
11, 9, 7, 5, 3, 1

About the Author

Michelle Ahern Bevans is a writer, poet and author of *Counting You to Pieces*, her first published collection of poetry. Living in a small coastal town south of Sydney, Australia – Michelle's passion for writing started at a young age as she discovered the powerful tool of using coded language to hide her diary secrets from her older sister.

For over two decades she has continued to write – crafting non-fiction short stories, essays and articles. While her professional work in Communications keeps writing central in her life, her love of rhythm and language have kept poetry at the heart of her work where she delves into themes of loss, authenticity, femininity and existence.

www.ingramcontent.com/pod-product-compliance
Lightning Source LLC
LaVergne TN
LVHW090039080526
838202LV00046B/3874